TIGHT BINDINGS

First published in 2024
Published by Puncher and Wattmann
PO Box 279
Waratah NSW 2298
https://www.puncherandwattmann.com
web@puncherandwattmann.com

ISBN 9781923099210

Edited by Ed Wright
Cover illustration: Zom Osborne www.zomosborne.com
Cover design and typesetting: Miranda Douglas www.mirandadouglas.com
Printed by Lightning Source International

NATIONAL
LIBRARY OF AUSTRALIA

A catalogue record for this book
is available from the National Library of Australia.

Australian Government | **Creative Australia**

This project has been assisted by the Australian Government through Creative Australia, its principal arts investment and advisory body.

TIGHT BINDINGS

Sarah Temporal

Puncher & Wattmann

CONTENTS

TRANSFORMING

THREE SECRETS

I did not give birth to my daughter.
After labouring two days, three long nights,
she was trapped in the tight bindings of my body.
A doctor cut through to release her—

       maybe that doctor gave birth to my daughter.

There were dozens of people
who climbed from their beds in dim night and
converged on the fluorescent beacon of the hospital
to invite my baby into that white air—

       maybe they all gave birth to my daughter.

I surrendered to the table, made a kind of peace.
Lines ran into my outstretched arms
and a blue curtain dismembered
the lower half of my senses while

       the scalpel gave birth to my daughter.

My baby's heart was steady as a drum
until she rose up stunned
through that surprising doorway

       as if she gave birth to herself—

when I could not. All I gave
were these inadequate
thanks.

II.

Later, I could not stop chasing the story of myself.
I found my likeness as the mother of Asclepius
when he was extracted from my body—

       a myth gave birth to my daughter.

I found   my earliest survival in 1580   my husband
took a knife to me   the husband was a pig-farmer
and I lived on, nameless.   Even after   the invention of anaesthetic
they sometimes refused to use it   because God said,

      Woman Must Suffer to Bring Forth Children.

I found   a woman upon whose body
history has carved   a thousand notches   to remember every
incremental breakthrough.   She is supine in stone   in bas-relief
in charcoal drawings   always lifeless and naked   with all her secrets
spilled out on the ground.
It turns my stomach to look at her
but I have to—

      it is she
      in her endless stillness
      who gave birth to my daughter.

III.

They lay my baby down beside me.
Her tiny nose   presses my cheek
her eyes   seek me out
like she
has given birth
to me.

Watch the author reading
'Three Secrets'.

BREAKING / BECOMING

as if she gave birth
to herself

Watch the author reading
'Blackheath'.

BLACKHEATH

It's not right to be awake late at night, here:
there's secret business down in the gully
between the darkness and the trees

and it must be obeyed. So I wait until
the morning's walk to bear news of our liaison
to the discerning ferns. My skin carries

your heat. Daring stringybarks shed
their robes, and discard them in heaps
at their feet. They step lithely down to the creek,

dip their toes in the cool dark water.
(Sometimes we find they have died in the night,
and fallen headlong into it.) And today,

the wet old chopping block is splintered
to bits. I stand on the deck and watch clouds
whip themselves black, and you speak me

that impossible verse, twisting your beanie
to a furball in your nervousness. Nobody
intervenes. But night falls again

on Blackheath. So we follow
the law of the storm
the way the beasts keep each other warm.

IN THE KIMBERLEY

There are certain things you should learn
before going out bush. How to kill a big fish
quickly, being one. Mouths get caught

no matter who casts the line. Someone needs
to own it. The station-owner asks offhand
could we check the hooks he left down that way,

a track sticky with compacted dust pulling
us along, together but alone. My mind
dissociates in this elemental heat. We find

the lines crossing the creek: giant
spider-threads, discarded death-traps
lankly billowing. Looks like nothing. Then—

crashing into air— the gaping milk-bottle mouth
of a big Barra breaks the mud-brown surface apart.
And we see that it is nearly spent. Its hours

of torment belong to us now: small-time
big-city pacifists on a road-trip to seek out
Australia, not looking too closely at our own

mismatched hearts. We haul in our unlucky
catch. Massive thrash of writhing metal,
heavy as a mallet, one whole metre long.

My lover's face sets in grim distaste. He locates
the gills, slides the blade in where he thinks
the brain must be. Declares, *That's him then.*

But it isn't. Welling blobs of scarlet shimmy
the sides of the gasping fish and still it fights
and fights, it survives a second stabbing, unites

us on the banks of our failure. I walk away
when asked to, only to spare him the shame.
The water knows it, licking clean.

The fish makes a feast for twenty people
back at camp. We ask the men there— hard
men, their compact knowledge guarded

like rolled tobacco— what we should
have done? *Bleed it from the throat next time,*
they say. *It dies slow, tastes better.*

LAMEROO

On this beach   your sight doesn't count for much
perceive with touch   and stillness
take refuge in fat-leaved mangrove shade
    take refuge in humid decay
        hide inside the gust that whispers   storm coming

        Sit cross-legged, height of termite-mound
        cotton shorts gape from waist   sweat drips on bone-tight skin
        you like this body too-thin   nothing between you and the grating sky
the salt-rot-syrup scent   manic city's edge   everything here is in a hurry to dissolve, so spill
        your liquid centre   disclose this bayou to strangers
            they are kind   they say it passes

Cast your sadness into the ocean   the ocean brings it back
    men call to each other in language   they throw handlines into the water
        tradies sink tinnies after work   cargo ships hang from the horizon
        return here every morning   return in the cling-wet evening
            stay until the dragonflies swarm   touch nerves of the earth with scarlet wings
                        be   still

Pretend that all this stays when you go   let the sea wrap you in her skirts of blue

let hunger recall you to your body

           and when the storm snaps overhead

                                    get up and   leave.

How to move into a caravan, age 29

place your caravan in a field
in the country
far away
from where your adult life is unfolding

furnish it
with things you left behind when
you moved out the first time

your bookshelf should hold
no more than two books
otherwise, there will be thinking

once you're settled
write a letter to those who could have been
your parents-in-law. Don't
wait for a reply

now that you don't own anything to speak of
never carry keys
keys are for real people
not for you.

FIVE PICTURES OF MY FATHER CHOPPING WOOD

I.

My father chops wood
like nobody
has ever been injured by an axe.

In the moment before
metal strikes, everything
is airborne.

He brings it down
and all the way through
as if he simply looked
into tree-flesh and said,
Break.

So it springs apart.
The halves dive sideways
off the block and I notice

it is this. This
is what I must describe
about my father.

II.

He casts the axe into air
like other men cast fishing lines.
As if it weighs nothing.
I remember him listening, never commenting,
only ever listening when I told him my thoughts.
Listening with absolute attention.
As if my blundering, incomplete child's mind
was never awkward for him to hold.
As if it weighed nothing.

III.

This should be a messier business than it is.
The swiftness of the blow leaves little room for error.
I must be watching this from
the loungeroom window,
or over the fence in the crisp winter air.
It must have been in that time when I
returned to their house in pieces
pretending to be whole
and knotty enough to withstand
almost every attempt to break the truth
out of me.

IV.

There is no aggression,
no strain in his actions.
He simply invites the wood to become
what it always was.

I write now as if he is gone. He isn't;
he had a bypass only last year,
in the Royal Prince Alfred on Missenden Road
while I used my hotel room and heightened emotions
to finish poems like this.
He was too tall to ever get comfortable
in the hospital bed.

V.

The axe sings to the air
with the clarity
of a single cloudless thought.

I remember my father chopping wood
more frequently than I ever watched him do it.
There was something about that swing of the axe.
It was nobody else's business.

CLOSE TO THE SKY

A performance poem

We live close to the sky.

Its hot wet breath   gathers itself on the mountainside   flicks clothes from the line
lifts wisps of our hair   then tumbles itself into storm   lumbers down to the beach
and dumps its secrets in the sea   while we fill brimming cups of our eyes.

There are those who see in our contentment   a kind of failure.
Truth is, I see no cause to invite abundance into my life   when I already have everything that I need.

Now I unravel these country roads   in my fossil-fuelled solitude.
I follow them back   to the place we met   at the halfway interlude
between the furthest you could climb   on splintered lungs   and dwindling time
and my limited will to know that I   must reach the summit alone.

In the intimacy of this truth   I fell for you— at least they always call it falling
but surely we were   rising in love.

16

Now we live close to the sky   and I fold these landscapes into my mind:
these hills slick with cloud-spit   these sudden egrets spraying sky.
None of it exists outside of time   in this life of not-quite.

But I think this might be enough for me
if it is enough for you.

We live
close to the sky

and tend to a garden of blue.

17

$\mathcal{A}$ND THEN

in the deep moisture of a subtropical / night in August / we both know / it is time for our bodies to meet / as we clean our teeth / I rehearse / my breathless fear / that you will be weak and worn out / that your skin will be clammy / that you won't reach me / yours is a body I can't read / it is closed and enclosed / in presupposition / in warnings / in social quarantine / I fear / that the story of this night will be / that I love you but lovemaking is merely endurable / yet I can't keep my hands off you / as we slide into sheets and the creek pulls darkness over its sleek / uninhibited progress and you touch me like / reaching the sun on the other side / of the earth you are all right there / surging to the surface of your thin limbs / you kiss like wild ginger / pushing against the moon / your touch is like / depth charges in / open ocean / a soundless / booming / over and over / it is still felt / in my depths / right now / years later / where I try to trace the imprint of us / in a language / tainted by horror of sickness / tainted by saviours with other agendas / than the pure thundering desire / that leaps over my tact / as I forget / to love you tender but press / your light frame with my full weight / as I consume your salt and vinegar sweat / and your sweet tenacious breath / I / climb toward / you / hand over hand / wrapping your DNA around my wrist / making my way along your genetic chains / seeking out a language that is worthy / of touching your body / when all our words have been spent / on the ways that you are incomplete / when they tell me you are ailing / emaciated / hunched / infected / and my pleasure says: *English, you're drunk! Go home!* / and all my nerves and organs rise in fury to inscribe / this passion upon its absence / here where our bodies meet as equals / here where you pull away gasping for air / where infirmity and eros have / the same oceanic eyes / where language leaves us to this / slow stroking of soft / white curtains / blowing over our bodies / at dawn

18

AFTER THE TRANSPLANT

I.

My mind
          bucks away
from the image of your cage wide open

as if the white dove might flap free
even in retrospect
if my thoughts go there.

Your body
too quickly put back together,
a resurrection too sudden
to comprehend, and now

you are perfect. You sleep
released from the memory
of your body's wreck.

II.

When you were beyond my reach
in the operating theatre, in the hands of those
superbly skilled and caring men, and I
waited—
with the marshmallow couches and the
inane films playing soundlessly,
I had a vision of them— of us— humans
practising such feats upon each other.
Holding one of our own, so precisely,
so thoughtfully, in relation to death,
that the edge between life and no-life fragmented
and dispersed into so many tiny actions, weights and attentions,
into such a myriad of forms,
that it seemed impossible to lose you after all.

III.

They told me
you were bleeding— a lot—
or too much— I could not
any longer detect
the story behind
kind intentions.

IV.

They had distributed for safe-keeping
all your life's energy among a huge forest
of machinery puffing and pulsing:
your breath transferred to a pumping bellows,
your heartbeat relocated to a cave-like screen
on which other lines ran, gold, blue and green.

An ecosystem composed
of human brilliance
and compassion.

V.

I saw you held
in steady hands, close
to the mystery. Slowly,

each fleck and pulse
was returned to you,
the cage doors wired shut.

You could not have known
how well you were. Yet
when your eyes opened,

it was you
who smiled first.

SINGING

*a myth that gave birth
to my daughter*

BIRTH MANTRA

A performance poem

Consider the miracle of birth:
A hole the size of a twenty-cent piece
That admits something five times its girth!
No one knows how it fits through our tight private bits
We're googling for all that we're worth.
As you picture the tearing, the stretching and swearing,
A logical panic ensues.
But I know that mine will be perfectly fine:
      My vagina is fucking huge.

In birth class they tell us, *Natural is best!*
And I'm always a straight-A student.
So I learn affirmations and visualisations
For A-grade vaginal improvements.
They say words have the power to shape our reality
(I'm hoping my words shape a massive new cavity)
As I plaster my walls with gargantuan fannies
And visualise yonis you could drive a truck through.
I chant and I pray, repeat ten times a day:
      My vagina is fucking huge.

In the birth suite, the midwife peers in with a frown,
And her words come back out with an echoey sound:
This one is the roomiest I've ever seen!
The doctor leans forward, then trips and falls in.
She pulls him out dripping and looking confused
As he meekly confirms, *M'am, in medical terms,*
      Your vagina is fucking huge.

It's enormous, it's vast, it's immense!
A megalomaniac's flapping wet tent!
Maybe yours is a rose, or a lady-garden;
Mine's like a dozen-lane autobahn
My babies whizz down it and win the Grand Prix!
It runs on high-octane hyperbole:
It's a racetrack, a ski slope, an Olympian luge!
　　　Fucking hell! This vagina is huge.

But—
it's only as big as it needs to be.
It reaches from here to eternity
Channelling souls into uterine seas
Escorting humans from nothing to being.
Our hopes for the future, our fears and our love,
The vagina delivers them all.
This must have been what men feared when they told us,
Vaginas should always be small.
But high-fiving sizes and boasting of bigness
Was never exclusive to those with a penis.
Time to reclaim! Will you join me and say:
　　　Vaginas are FUCKING HUGE!

GROWTH CYCLE

The growth of daughters is cyclic, and forms nests over time. Within the family home, an intermediate plenty of mould, known as shower, occurs between the mother and Tuesday. Between 85 and 90% of daughters are reading their futures at any one time. In the hours between school and dinner, abundant pieces of fruit, paper, and attention form the new daughter, pushing out the old inactive daughter as the new one advances. The book bindings, peeling back to reveal the new daughter, multiply rapidly and ascend into picturesque togetherness. The visible daughter is composed of outer branches, the woman and, sometimes, a world of peace. It may be difficult to identify which phase each daughter occupies: a nest of trees, all of which are made of story.

CROOKED MAN

there was a crooked man
who lived in a crooked house
he thought he was a winner
but he had his crooked doubts

he found a crooked wife
married in a crooked church
and did a crooked job
every time he went to work

he had a crooked past
living with a crooked dad
who'd used a crooked stick
for every feeling that he had

so this crooked little man
as he walked a crooked mile
took it out in crooked comments
on the girls who wouldn't smile

he met his crooked mates
and they shared their crooked schemes
for winning back their precious rights
to live their crooked dreams

he turned a crooked corner
he bought a crooked van
he drove a crooked road
cooking up a crooked plan

he finds the time upon him
she's standing there alone
the truest thing he's ever laid
his crooked eyes upon

beneath a crooked moon
all his worry disappears
he's found a crooked way
to feel less crooked than he is

he sighs a crooked sigh
buckles up his crooked belt
and he takes a crooked picture
to remember how he felt

now he's striding like a hero
never falters when he stops
to discuss a crooked question
with the local crooked cop

the papers are all brimming
with his many crooked flaws
they know we'll never catch him
with our crooked little laws

and I've told this crooked story
though it isn't mine to tell
tried to change my crooked thinking
—oh! it isn't going well

I have heard his crooked comments
I have felt his crooked touch
I have walked his crooked line between
too little and too much

it's a crooked kind of lucky
that with all his good advice
I have only been assaulted
once in all my crooked life

I wish I could just rise above
my crooked view of them
but if you're taught to fear the dark
I guess you start to bend

I still flash my crooked keys
still adjust my crooked hems
and it's still my job to be the one
who fixes crooked men.

THE GRAVEYARD

Your hair twisted up, pinned with flowers
You pick your way forward alone
You have the same face as a woman
Who lies under one of these stones.

The lace of the sunlight through branches
The dim glow that touches her name
The years that snake mute through the bracken
The vines stitched to tree-trunks like hems.

And eucalypts filter the dead song
Of cutters and pioneer's wives
And infants lie coiled there like snails' shells
Too young to know they were alive.

They dream that you've come there to find them
Still wearing their dead mother's face
Their arms raise in mute expectation
To be gathered up from their graves.

You'd comfort and kiss them and hold them
As no one has done for so long
You'd rock them to sleep with the memory
Of warm skin enfolding their bones.

But your own child, who's brazenly living
Commands you to hurry back up
You barely beg pardon to scramble
Through dense scrub and ferns to the top.

31

You climb past the bush rock inscriptions
The scribbly gums forging laments
Past broad-leafed things riddling up gravestones
Past moss-covered iron and cement.

Return to the dusk where your daughter
Stands balanced like time on the gate
Until someday the clay calls you homeward
And she'll bear the dead woman's face.

TRANSFORMING

*like she
has given birth
to me*

THE RISING

She answered, "Dear father, do with me what you will. I am your child," and with that
she stretched forth both hands and let her father chop them off.
— 	Jacob and Wilhelm Grimm, 'The Girl Without Hands'.

This daughter is rising, wearing
armour she made from the skin of a flea.
She shelters flames in her pelvic cave
and kicks with her ink-black feet.

She rises out of every story
that stuttered her like a moth in a glass:
her weightless limbs beat and beat like nothing
could thunder harder than this page.

Other daughters rise up from altars,
rise from tree-trunks and beds. This one
prises open the fist that collected
her, lips red as blood, red as murder.

They are coming unbound and unbidden,
these daughters, going out dressed as the moon.
They spit out penalties and prohibitions
that had stained their tongues with ash.

Look: these daughters are grown. They gather
all the children and limbs they have lost.
They press their voices back into their chests.
They carry dead hands in their canine teeth.

All of your daughters are rising now, see:
rising like embers, like flames. May the sound
of their blazing in the tongue-drunk night
stir you softly in your grave.

Watch the author reading
'The Rising'.

Now squash the egg!

The giant who has no heart in his body
      gets stuck for words when he likes a girl
      marks himself up with a brag-map of tatts
      crushes out ciggies in old growth forests
      flutters the lashes of his mother's eyes
      twigs that the system is rigged and he's winning
      stakes a forearm in the table every time he talks
      calls you snowflake
      calls you sweetheart
      calls you late at night
      likes you better with your hair long
      sleeps with both fists closed
      wakes to hear enemies pounding the gates
      cries silently into open-cut mines
      shields himself with saviour-shaped women
      quotes from the book of his father, of all giants:
      I hid my heart in a place you'll never find it
      and no one does, until they do.

The giant who had no heart in his body
      crumples like a tinnie, falls flat.
      Falls into forest,
      into memory,
      forms a small, lumpy hill,
      that no one sees the need to fence off.

And people still climb it to this day,
      with their shovels, listening for a tick.

WILD AND TANGLED

Under a powder-blue sky with drifting smoke   there's a back road that no one has cause to take   A fence
with leafless rosebushes   skulls of steers guard the gate   The house is ringed with rambling sheds
where heavy, sharp, and grinding tools are kept   A garden wild and tangled, flecked   with flight of red-
capped fairy wrens   And you have heard   here lives the beast.

He has such shining fur, such shining eyes   so diamond-sharp and pale   You think you've never seen
anything so male   Everybody wants to touch him   shygirls-oldwomen-straightmen, everyone   wants to
tangle handfuls of that mane   Those gleaming claws appeared no more   than fine, articulate fingers
The way he looked at you and saw   the blood that beat beneath your skin   seemed evidence of grace
All you want to do is follow   every rippling cloud across his face   Wrap yourself in muscle   Sleep on
growling chest   And you think   you are the only woman   who's tucked herself into his house   drunk
the beer he handed you and thought   *He is my life now*   with quiet thrill.

You don't believe a thing they say in town   Besides, those shunning only serve to harden   beastly natures
of their own   And look how he has time for all of them   Lavishes feasts of smile and wit   Makes
angelic visitations   Spreads his redolent length upon the verandas of the lonely   He is huge   enough to
make up for your smallness   He protects you   and you are scared.

38

The dream is to reveal   what he is hiding under clothes   Perhaps the good man he grows to be   Perhaps
rank pelt   wafts of sweet manure, sticky burrs, sweat and fear   It's you alone can lick and soothe and clean
away that fear   Your roots hold fast   You weather droughts   with your wordless friends   They flit
about, the little wrens   with drops of blood bright on their heads   You're nothing like those other women
who he tore apart   For you have read the story   Transformation at its heart   where beast becomes
human   and human, beast.

Then it is only a sign of intimacy and trust   to hear at night   The cries of swallows in his garden, crushed
whose nests he batted down with thwacking paws   The cries of cattle whose sides he slashed   and left a
bloody feast for flies   Or the cries of wallaby whose graceful necks he snapped   dragged hot fur on the
forest floor   And the rumours of women   to whom he did all of this   and more.

I do not mean to say that nature cannot change   I saw you stray   on that road, the stones obscured utterly
with bracken   Where his scent lay thick with spreading, powerful warmth   And it is far, far too easy to say
that we must simply know our value   refuse to be his prey   You would not be called away   Nor should
the burden of that choice be yours   Perhaps his transformation is only ever wrought   beneath the teeth of
other beasts   their particular smoke-and-fire talk   Not by all the heroic strength with which   you followed
his twitching tail   into the scrub

escorted by flashing reptiles and   the startled flight of birds

UNDER THE SOIL

Once there were two brothers two brothers in a book in a child's bedroom the child in the farmhouse sleeping or not sleeping much the child is having nightmares now the child is grown up the two brothers went to hunt a dangerous boar for the king's reward the brothers rode forth *you go that way* said the cowardly older brother *I will go this* the younger brother never returns the murder goes undiscovered year upon year rain after rain the bones lay silent until the country was returned to its people the mountain where spirits step off to meet the dead the land was always returning to its stories the river rich and dark the child wakes in the farmhouse and cannot name the sound that woke her the bones are discovered they are brought before the king the bones have been fashioned into a flute the bones sing murder the flute holds the tune of the brother's betrayal while the child is digging dark rich river soil finds farmdog ex-wallaby cow jawbone little skull piece of shin they come to the surface after rain the soil has secrets that are only given up to children sing of dispossession sing of slavery the child is a woman now the woman returns home the land returns to its people the fact is fashioned into conscience the bones sing of murder sing of slavery sing of the inheritance they gave to me the child in the farmhouse never can sleep the bones cannot sing the truth into our mouths

UNBROKEN

I remember, Cinderella
How you were just thirteen when you first tried to escape.
You painted red nails, red lips, zipped yourself up. Said, *Fuck it. I'm going to the ball.*

I remember how dangerous you seemed
You came home and no one knew where you'd been
How your body was a weapon
How your body seemed to know too much
How your body was the only thing the fairy godmother had to give you
How you made your own ballgowns out of spite
How you wanted to stay out the whole damn night
How you danced! Long and hard in shoes made of glass—
     improbable and breakable as your heart— you wore
     those contradictions with such grace they somehow never broke
How you didn't even cry when you finally spoke.

I remember, Cinderella
When you said *boyfriends* but you meant men: ten times our size and terrifying
How you were waging a war of attraction
How you deployed eyeliner and vodka to make yourself appear taller
How they seemed docile as cattle while you herded them in
How their hooves left bruises on your skin.

I remember, Cinderella
How you scratched sharp poems in a language no one else could read
You hid the truth under a two-dollar-shop figurine—
You knew the value of appearing worthless.

I remember, Cinderella
Your gaze was steady on the day you told me your home had never been safe
How you were born into a spell of silence
How somebody tossed your childhood into the dark like a cheap toy
How you kept asking older men to help you find it
How your diary was inscribed on the inside of your skin
How you thought when they entered you they might catch a glimpse
And you wished just one of them would turn out to be the prince—

They never were. And now I see
How you made it out at last, quietly brushing ashes out of your hair
How you raise your children right
How you survived
You chucked those old glass shoes, let them splinter and subside
(We are older now, barefoot, and so much harder
to break).
And I hear you still dance, sometimes,
in the opening cracks of the night.

Watch the author reading
'Unbroken'.

Rapunzel

I. The Maiden in the Tower

Who is this?

Someone who cannot remember her mother.
Growing up in circles, every day the same,
inside the single wall that binds
a speck of longing inside her name: *Rapunzel*,
she whispers. Calls herself up by the roots.
See her walking the tower round:
a stylus of want, skirting the stifled air,
she shrugs semi-darkness around her shoulders
as mosquitoes delve and pry, siphon her rage—
the nights are hardest. By day, there's a green
view of things she never touched,
heat rises into the towering dome,
eucalypts exhale their fug into her face.
Days loop back into lethargy, circle around
like stacks of books that line the walls,
remind her there's no point chasing
bush-mice out of the cracks, no point
building shelves for all these books.
She has tried dressmaking and weaving too,
drinking and baking and masturbating.
See how hollow it is, this fort of solitude?
How filled with her, how empty?

II. *The Hair*

is most outrageous
and familiar.

Hair stuck in her mouth,
caught round her wrists,
hair piled over the bed.
Heaping tragic haystack of hair,
clownish girl-child's fantasy of hair,
dragging, lagging, bridal train of hair,
rustling shadows: she turns to face
her mute pursuer, never there.
Sweeping, sinful, susurrous hair,
wallowing, weighty, insomniac hair,
circles painted with a wake of hair,
enormous snake of hair that could
swallow her whole where she sleeps.
A burden of hair. An aching of hair.
A mess of a festering excess of hair.
A cumulant sensual swelling of hair.
A cellular, seeking, intelligence paired
with confinement. There—
the question I never closed—
did the seed of that growth
form in the tower, or
create itself in her?
In her body?

III. *Bindings*

I see her. You see her.
Girl locked in tower.
Girl locked out of reach of her own power.

I see her. I sense her.
I want to tell the story with feelings,
not words.

I sense her. I seek her.
A long and snakelike tale, winding
through four long centuries.

They seek her. I see her.
Around the edges of her mind
run stone-cold rings of doubt.

She sees me. I hear her.
If only I were normal
They would surely let me out.

They seek her. They write her.
Hunted down, caught
and bound.

They write her. I find her.
Borne by male hands
like spoils of war.

They bind her. They bind her.
Her mystery becomes
scalp. Becomes trophy.

You see her. I see her.

IV. Landscape

Her only landscape is her hair. She disappears
into its windings and hollows, its forests
and creeks. A strand for every day
of her stopped-off
life.

V. Portrait

She has always reflected
what we wanted to see
                    Rapunzel. Rampion. Prunella.
in dainty illustrations
patient, painted maiden
                    Blond Beauty. Parsillette.
golden hair cascades down
she waits to be saved
                    The fair Angiola. Petrosinella.
docile smile
                    Persinette.
enclosed spaces
                    Clothilde.
see the woman with a thousand faces
                    Uzembeni. Danaë. Antonia. Justine.
replicated over years and generations
                    Bond girl. Lois Lane. Princess Peach. Diana.
somehow the story never changes
and even I repeat
the same archaic phrases

I can see no way out
of my situation.

VI. *Desire*

Biology grinds and burns.
I pace the tower in my turn,
having chosen a jawline to trust,
a chest to bury myself in.

Biology grinds and burns.
Rapunzel's hair stirs.
Basile names it a golden banner
streaming from the tower,

calling the prince to enlist
in the army of love. Allow me
this moment of fantasy:
as they lay there, sated, spent,

for once in her life, the hair
just stopped.

VII. *Exile*

Where you cannot break out,
you may simply break.

Or perhaps, become something
the story cannot hold.

Her belly is swelling, her body telling
a secret that cannot be contained

spilling beyond the edges of hems and margins
and into the face of propriety— the Grimms

replace her pregnancy with a very ladylike
stupidity— either way, it is enough to get her

thrown out. I see her fall—
unborn life and all—

into the obscurity of those lost years
where she births alone in the wilderness:

twins, who cling to her, knowing
she has been forgotten by her own

story. The lover likewise suffers,
wandering to find her, blind, his eyes

torn out on thorns. And of course,
her hair has been shorn—

innocent no more.

VIII.   Hope

is when she exits page left   and I cannot see her   a story that grabs
you doesn't end you just stop telling it   all of this happened so many
times ago that if you counted you would have to borrow some from the
children   I don't want to forget the beginning when the earth and sea
were new he drove me home and a very good time it was too   but a
prince shared by many is half a prince and I was not at all sorry for what I
swore would be the last word   Rampion is an autogamous plant it will
curl like braids or coils on a maiden's head   fertilising itself the story
unravels when observed   it was not until yours that my word tune was
formed   *Rapunzel, Rapunzel, let it come, let it go*

IX. Return

My daughter peers intently
through the windowing page
through dainty illustrations
and archaic phrasing

something stirs
something waiting
stretched taut and straining
to break free

who is this
who fills me
creates herself in this
untold body

I tuck in her covers
smooth her soft mane
touch each century I waited
to learn her name

then step into the wholeness
of her dreaming night

in her doorway, leave
a single strand of light.

Watch the author reading
'Rapunzel'.

NOTES

Three Secrets Historical references "Caesarian section: a brief history" pamphlet, National Library of Medicine. https://www.nlm.nih.gov/exhibition/cesarean/index.html

Growth cycle was created from found text including "Physiology, hair" (https://www.ncbi.nlm.nih.gov/books/NBK499948/). Part of the writing process employed text manipulation through Glass Leaves 2.0 www.leaves.glass

The rising owes a creative debt to Tishani Doshi.

Now squash the egg! references the fairy tale about a giant who removed his heart from his body and hid it in an egg. The title comes from a version by Klara Stroebe, "Anent the Giant Who Did Not Have His Heart About Him", https://www.surlalunefairytales.com/

Under the soil is stylistically influenced by Ania Walwicz. It draws on the fairy tale "The Singing Bone", from *Household Tales by Jacob and Wilhelm Grimm* https://www.surlalunefairytales.com/

Rapunzel

'winding through four long centuries': literary versions of the Rapunzel story appear from the 1600s onwards in Europe. Jack Zipes, 2001, *The Great Fairy Tale Tradition*. (Norton).

'Basile': Giambattista Basile's "Petrosinella", published in 1634.

'The Grimms replace her pregnancy': In Schulz' and de la Force's earlier versions of the tale, the witch discovers that Rapunzel is pregnant by the prince, and expels her from the tower in consequence. However, the Grimms (1857) eliminated references to sexual intercourse, instead having Rapunzel 'blurt out' her secret.

'all of this happened so many [years] ago that if you counted [on your fingers] you would have to borrow some from the children' is a traditional ending from Folktales of the Amur. https://internationalstoryteller.com/folktale-and-fairy-tale-endings/

'[in] the beginning when the earth and sea were new' is a popular oral tale opening. https://internationalstoryteller.com/folktale-and-fairy-tale-beginnings/

'[A story, a story,] let it come, let it go' is a traditional West African opening for oral tales. *Ib id.*

'Rampion is an autogamous plant... curl like braids or coils on a maiden's head' (Thompson 1989). Annotations for *Rapunzel*, https://www.surlalunefairytales.com/h-r/rapunzel/rapunzel-tale.html

ᴀCKNOWLEDGEMENTS

This work was created on the lands of the Bundjalung nation where I now live. I was born on the lands of the Jerrinja people. I acknowledge the traditional owners of these unceded lands and waters, and pay respect to Elders past and present.

Poems in this collection first appeared (sometimes in earlier versions) in the following journals and publications: *Australian Poetry Anthology*, *Cordite Poetry Review*, *Meniscus*, *Verity La.*, *Heroines Anthology*, *Not-Very-Quiet*, *Social Alternatives*, and *Rochford St Review*. 'Three secrets' was shortlisted for the Val Vallis Award and the South Coast Writers Centre Poetry Prize. The audio-poems based on 'Crooked Man' and an earlier version of 'Three secrets' were shortlisted for the Arts Queensland XYZ Prize for Innovation in Spoken-word. I thank the editors and producers for these opportunities that encouraged me to share my work.

Thanks to my mentor Melinda Smith, whose advice and encouragement kept my imposter syndrome at bay long enough to finish this book. Thanks also to editor Matilda Gould for early input on thematic connections, and for making my words more comfortable on the page.

Thanks are also due to Zom Osborne for creating the artwork for *Tight Bindings*, a generous and joyful collaboration. Thanks to Miranda Douglas for the cover design and typesetting and to Ed Wright for editing and publishing this book.

To everyone who supported my work in large and small ways, I thank you: Kerri Shying, Esther Ottaway, Es Foong, Miriam Hechtman, Matt Hetherington, Toni Wills, Gillian Swain, Janette Hoppe, Caroline Reid, Andrew Gray, Brooke Scobie, Red Room Poetry, Queensland Poetry, Byron Writers Festival, The Bunker Spoken Word, Girls on Key, Word Travels, Red Dirt Festival, Melbourne Spoken Word, and so many more. Thanks to those who came out to listen; to the baristas of Bacaro for fuelling my Saturday morning writing sessions; and to my Poets Out Loud community for taking my little passion and giving it back tenfold.

I gratefully acknowledge the support of Create NSW in the development of this work.

Finally, thanks to my husband Damien, for co-creating writing residencies inside family life; and to my daughter Harriet who is a creative spark.

This project was supported by the NSW Government through Create NSW.

$\mathcal{A}$BOUT THE AUTHOR

Sarah Temporal was born on Jerrinja lands on the NSW South Coast and now lives on Bundjalung country in Murwillumbah. *Tight Bindings* is her first published poetry collection, arriving twenty years after she first took the stage as a shy, socially awkward poet-to-be. Since then, she has performed her work Australia-wide. In recent years she has transformed and published poems for the page, prompted partly by the constraints of parenthood and pandemic lockdowns. She has always been fascinated by the power of poetry to reveal our hidden selves.

Sarah's work has appeared in *Best of Australian Poetry* and been shortlisted for the Val Vallis Award. She has been a finalist three times for the Arts Queensland XYZ Prize for Excellence in Spoken Word. Her wins include the 2021 Bunker Slam and 2018 Nimbin Performance Poetry World Cup, and winning the very first national poetry slam in Australia with her team in 2006. She has collaborated with circus artists and musicians, and completed a residency with Queensland Poetry where she was mentored by Joelle Taylor.

With a background in education, Sarah has taught poetry to hundreds of people from ages 8 all the way to 89, and now runs the regional arts initiative Poets Out Loud to empower voices of all ages. Her particular passion for working with teens led her to establish the Youth Slam for the Northern Rivers in partnership with Byron Writers Festival. She curates and hosts performance events, and mentors young and emerging writers.

She lives with her husband Damien, who is also a poet and lives with cystic fibrosis, and daughter Harriet. She dreams of one day being the proud owner of a clean shower and getting a good night's sleep.